The Story of
Adventure Santa

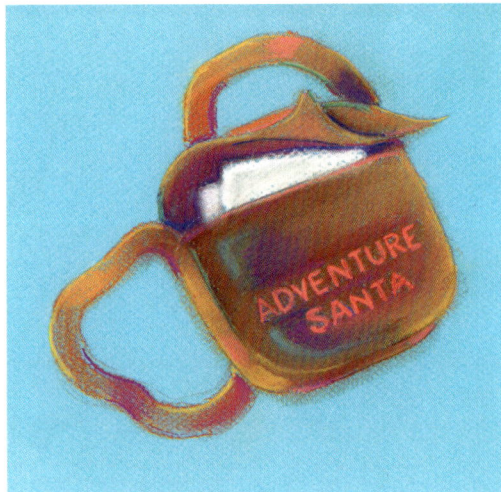

Story by Sean and Catherine Green
Written by Megan Borgert-Spaniol
Illustrated by Kim Gordon

The Story of Adventure Santa

ISBN: 978-0-9979473-1-1

Printed in the United States of America.
Bang Printing, Brainerd, Minnesota

First Printing: 2016

10 9 8 7 6 5 4 3 2 1

Adventure Santa, LLC
adventuresanta.com

We dedicate this book and
Adventure Santa to our boys
Connor and Seamus –
We love you and look forward to a life filled
with many more adventures together!

It was the first of December, and the Christmas season had just begun. Far up in the snowy white world of the North Pole, Santa was settling in for a long afternoon.

As he surveyed the thousands of envelopes that had arrived that morning, he smiled to himself. Reading these letters from girls and boys, each filled with wishes and brimming with joy, was his favorite task of all. Sitting among the stacks, heaps, and bags full of messages from all over the world, Santa felt surrounded by love.

With the fireplace warming his toes and a mug of hot cocoa in hand, Santa stretched out on his most comfortable armchair and reached for the letter at the top of the nearest pile.

As he began to read, his eyes lit up. This note was not from a child; it was from the parents of two little children! Hearing from moms and dads always made Santa happy.

Dear Santa,

We are the parents of Keeley and Michael. We want to thank you for the joy you bring our family every year. We love to watch our kids fill with Christmas spirit. Their excitement is the greatest gift you give us, and it inspires us to celebrate the season as often as possible. We only wish we had more opportunities to make new memories as a family!

Thank you for all you do to bring the magic of Christmas into our homes.

With Love,
Keeley and Michael's mom and dad

Snowflakes swirled outside the window and the embers crackled at Santa's feet. The towers of letters shrank slowly over the afternoon as he read them, one by one. By the time darkness had fallen and the fire was burning low, Santa had read many more notes from parents just like Keeley and Michael's. They were all thanking him for the fun memories he helped their families create.

Santa laid his head back and closed his eyes. He began to imagine how he could bring these families more of the Christmas adventures they loved. His mind wandered to days long ago, when he would venture into the world without sleigh or red suit. Instead, he wore a backpack and a pair of sturdy hiking boots. That was all he needed to see the world and learn what Christmas meant to those who believed in its magic.

A rosy glow colored Santa's cheeks. These letters made him remember what he'd been missing. He wanted to bake gingerbread cookies, hang twinkle lights on evergreen trees, and sing carols at the neighbor's door. He wanted to join these families on their Christmas adventures.

An idea crept into Santa's mind. He couldn't abandon all the busy preparations at the North Pole, but perhaps there was still a way for him to take part in the family fun. Santa gulped the last of his cocoa and stood up. If this was going to work, he would need the help of his most trusted elf.

"Tavi? Can you spare a moment?" Santa asked as he tapped his head elf on the shoulder. He had found her in the workshop, hunched over the floor plan of a dollhouse and deep in concentration. When she looked up, her face immediately brightened.

"Anything for Santa," Tavi smiled.

Santa knew Tavi was as busy as ever, so he had to be quick. He told her about all the letters he'd received from parents and explained his own wish to take part in the holiday activities. Finally, he shared his great idea. When he finished, Santa pulled a photo from his pocket and gave it to Tavi.

"For inspiration," he winked.

Tavi worked through the night. She measured, cut, pasted, and stitched, only pausing now and then to glance at the photo Santa had given her. As the first morning light filtered through the frosted windows, the elf stood back and considered her finished product. With a satisfied nod and a great big yawn, Tavi set off to find Santa.

"Lords a-leaping, you've done it!" Santa whispered, his eyes wide with wonder. Before him stood a miniature model of himself, dressed exactly as he was in the photo he had given Tavi. A green shirt, red suspenders, and hiking boots: this is what Santa had worn to explore the world.

"Meet Adventure Santa," Tavi said. "He'll help bring Christmas memories to families around the world. And through him, you can be part of the fun."

Santa scratched his chin
and crinkled his brow. Tavi had
given him exactly what he needed.
But he still felt like something was missing.

With a smile that suggested she had read his mind,
Tavi cleared her throat.

"And now," she said, "the final touch." The elf
reached into her toolbox and pulled out a small
backpack. Santa gasped. It looked just like the pack he
had taken on his own expeditions.

"With this adventure pack, Adventure Santa can carry messages directly from you to the families," Tavi explained. "This is how you'll help them make the memories they're asking for!"

Santa beamed as Tavi carefully slipped the pack onto Adventure Santa's shoulders. When she stepped back, something magical happened. Adventure Santa came to life! With a joyful skip, he sprang from Tavi's table and landed on the ground.

"Ho-Ho, not so fast!" Santa laughed. He grabbed a piece of paper and wrote his first message:

Dear Keeley and Michael,

Are you ready for an adventure? Today, I'm feeling hungry for some sweets and would love to make sugar cookies with you. We can cut them into different shapes and decorate them with sprinkles and candies! Won't that be fun? Don't forget to ask your mom and dad for a little help. Let's get baking! Your friend, Santa

He placed the note in the backpack. Adventure Santa trembled with excitement to leave the workshop and see the world. His eyes darted between Santa and the door.

Santa couldn't help but chuckle. With a twinkle in his eye, he gave a nod. "Off you go, then."

And just like that, Adventure Santa was gone.

Since that day, Adventure Santa has been visiting the homes of families who wish to spend more time together. He waits for children and their parents to find him and open his backpack. Inside is a message from Santa with the next adventure.

Dear Keeley
and Michael,
Are you ready
for an adventure?
Today I'm feeling
hungry for some
sweets and would
love to make sugar
cookies with you.
We can cut them
into different shapes
and decorate them
with sprinkles and

21

With Adventure Santa by their sides, families all over the world set off on all kinds of Christmas adventures.

At the end of the day, the families are sleepy and full of new memories. Ready for bed, the kids and their parents say goodnight to Adventure Santa.

As they drift into their dreams, they wonder what adventures are in store for them next.

The

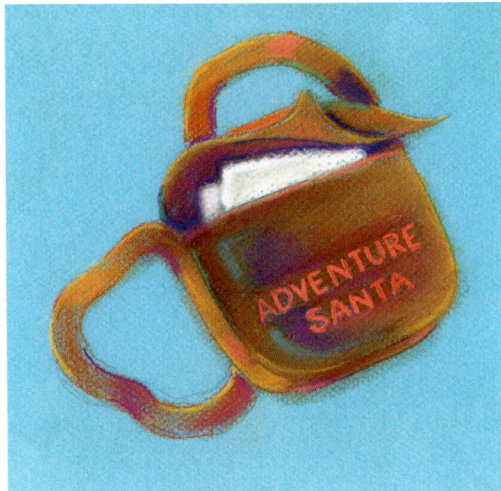

End

Note to Parents:

Welcome to the Adventure Santa Community, where our focus is on three things - **Fun • Family • Memories.** Adventure Santa creates an opportunity for intentional family time that the whole family can get excited about around familiar and new adventures.

For ideas, support and encouragement join the Adventure Community at **www.adventuresanta.com**. After joining, you will receive suggestions to continue to build **Fun • Family • Memories.**

www.adventuresanta.com